Permission to Settle

For Leslie,
with appreciation
for the generosity of
reading and inviting
me into your home—
Holly
5/24/26

Permission to Settle

Holly Flauto

Holly Flauto

ANVIL PRESS // VANCOUVER

Library and Archives Canada Cataloguing in Publication

Title: Permission to settle / poems by Holly Flauto.
Names: Flauto, Holly, author.
Identifiers: Canadiana 2024038640X | ISBN 9781772142389 (softcover)
Subjects: LCGFT: Poetry.
Classification: LCC PS8611.L395 P47 2024 | DDC C811/.6—dc23

Cover by Rayola.com
Interior layout: HeimatHouse
Represented in Canada by Publishers Group Canada
Distributed by Raincoast Books

The publisher gratefully acknowledges the financial assistance of the Canada Council for the Arts and the Province of British Columbia through the B.C. Arts Council.

Anvil Press Publishers Inc.
P.O. Box 3008, Station Terminal
Vancouver, B.C. V6B 3X5
www.anvilpress.com

Printed and bound in Canada.

For my Little Family:
Kevin, Joe and Franny

TABLE OF CONTENTS

12. Previous countries of residence: During the past five years have you lived in any country other than your country of citizenship or your current country of residence (indicated above) for more than six months? [ ] *No [ ] *Yes 41

13a. Your current marital status 43

13b. (If you are married or in a common-law relationship) Provide the date on which you were married or entered into the common-law relationship 45

13c. Provide the name of your current spouse / common-law partner 46

14a. Have you previously been married or in a common-law relationship? [ ]*No [ ]*Yes 47

14b. Provide the following details for your previous spouse / common-law partner: 48

14c. Type of relationship 49

14d. From / To 51

14e. Date of Birth 53

CONTACT INFORMATION

Current mailing address 54

Residential address 57

PASSPORT

1. Do you have a valid passport/travel document? [ ]*No [ ]*Yes 60
2. Country of issue 61
3. Issue date – Expiry date 62

NATIONAL IDENTITY DOCUMENT 64

EDUCATION/ OCCUPATION DETAIL

1. Highest level of education 66
2. Number of years of education in total 67
3. Current occupation 69
4. Intended occupation 72

LANGUAGE DETAIL

1. Native language / Mother Tongue 73

CANADA
10 CENTS

Establishing ACKNOWLEDGEMENT

I would like to acknowledge that
    I am writing today and
    I slept in a house last night
    on the traditional ancestral unceded territory of the
    xʷməθkʷəy̓əm, Sḵwx̱wú7mesh, and səlilwətat
    Nations

    I spend my work days
    on the traditional territory of the qiqéyt First Nation
    the only First Nation in Canada without a land base

I would like to acknowledge that
    I am asking to be Canadian
    to settle here and

I would like to acknowledge that
    I am asking the wrong people

    I am asking permission to settle
    from other settlers
    asking to join something I know is wrong
    complicit for not calling them out

I would like to acknowledge that
    I want this so much

I would like to acknowledge that
I need to ask permission from the settlers
to settle on the land
I know is not ethically theirs

I would like to acknowledge that
I know this is wrong
my choice is to be complicit
or to leave this place

my little family feels safe here
the child now teen found peers
emotionally expressive and smart as sparklers

I would like to acknowledge that
I walk onto this stolen land while
I assert in a million white checkboxes
to the settlers
that I should live here

while I betray them
by asking
whether this land is theirs
to grant permission

I would like to acknowledge that
when my feet first touched land
now called Vancouver
I was greeted by xʷməθkʷəy̓əm welcome figures

I would like to acknowledge that
        I ignored them

I had another chance that night
        another place to show understanding by the exit
        two more figures
        carved in the Tla-o-qui-aht tradition
        stood to welcome guests to the land

I would like to acknowledge that
        I looked past them to find a taxi

I would like to acknowledge again that
        I am a settler who now knows what it means
        to ask to settle
        that act of colonialism
        by committing this act of colonialism
        this act of spending so much energy
        to ask the wrong people
        and be so terrified to ask the right

        my acknowledgement
        stands empty
        pointing it out feels callous

I would like to acknowledge that
        I am afraid to speak
        to have difficult conversations
        instead of looking for a white box answer

I would like to ask
        people whose ancestors belong here

I would like to acknowledge that
        I am working up to that now

I need to act
        instead of these phrases and fragments
        or this means nothing

I would like to acknowledge that
        I know I have no right to ask
        compassion from those who do not understand why
        guidance from those who do
        forgiveness from everyone

I would like to acknowledge that
        the answer may be no

DOCUMENT CHECKLIST:

Application for a Permanent Resident Card or Permanent Resident Travel Document

GENERIC APPLICATION FORM FOR CANADA

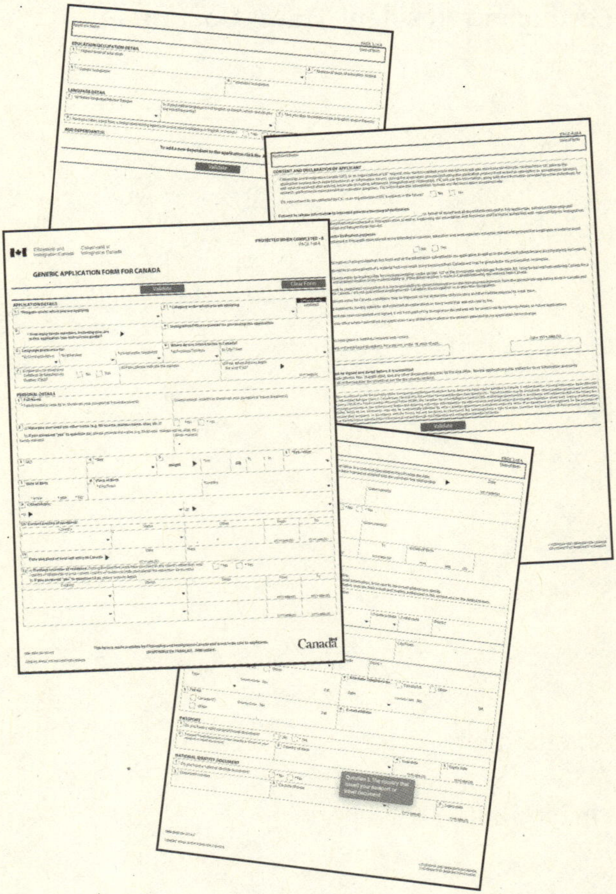

APPLICATION DETAILS

1. Program under which you are applying

I watch America
                                        collapse
from a desk in a third floor window

I watch America
                                        collapse

in a way I could not explain   to my brother
                                                  on the ground

I watch the towers of academia
                                                                  not fall
become taller so no one could reach   up
                                                                          or down
chambers of isolation and commerce

as far away as   the moons of Neptune and
echoing
                                                    echoing inside but not reaching
the harsh chain-smoking breath of summer

I watch instead of beholding a shovel
                                                                        or a saw
or a wrench and am grateful to be penned

as I watch
numbers
friends
family
lined up on bingo sheets

daub the cards firmly

hidden in attics and basements
survival rooms
the bingo I know will come
I know history
I know war
I know immigrant stories

whitewashed
like my own classic American fences
between leaving with family and dying
staying and waiting and dying
advocating in a non-dangerous way and dying
being those making change on the ground and dying
while I eviscerate words

and wait
watch the dying

2. Category under which you are applying

I am not yet a refugee
but the Romans fell and so will we
or they not me
and the destruction will be blood red
like baseball caps on white
letters and the poets will all die

family sponsorship is the right category
herculean for someone who still
aches and mends and frolics still
wearing the crash helmet of life
out of control of a narcissist
unrecognized dim flickers of eyelight
the trout dinners long ago thrown
in a compost bin

economic the economy of me and more
the teenager schooled only Canadian
who once defined privilege thus:
(pausing for a moment to put on his shoes)
riding three blocks with my mother
loading the car for her to protect her back
I carry a bag of dirt bought for seven dollars
for the succulents bought on clearance
on the way home from her work on the last day
before one of her months of vacation

3. How many family members including you, are in this application?

we are four
remove the two
already citizens
my partner current spouse
and the baby will be born here
and now was born

two
me my son

a yearning of three
me my son my mom
far away but all at home

a reverie of four
me my son my mom my dad
he exists here already
in dimes I find when I need them
a dime on a just-swept floor
a dime on the high windowsill of a new home on moving day
a dime on a desk in a hostile workspace
a dime in the drawer with the spoons
a dime stuck to the back of my phone
a dime on my bed
a dime on my son's bed
right after we've made them

officially two
plus one personal item that fits on the form in front of us

4. Immigration Office requested for processing this application

the one that understands what I do not say before I fail to say it
where I will be accepted for who I will never be

the one that matches the words without rhymes

the one that understands who I am not on the inside
and what I bring on picnic dinners

the one that thinks my potential faults
deserve survival kits and theme park rides

the one most likely to swipe right
and lean leftovers

5. Language preference for:
a) Correspondence b) Interview c) Interpreter requested

I want to hear your history in filigreed English
your family words for avocado and lawyer
how the language of who you have loved
races out of you foot after syllable
use the words for which English   has no words
and the ones who are done learning   can be done

I demand the use of opensource   English
academic English
is accented English   unaccessible
    biased English
    closed English
    limited English
    washed English
listen to the accent you did not hear
                                                            guarded by grammarians
                                                            and grandmothers
until voted out and conservatism
becomes tied to what has always been
instead of what it was when they were a child

we will misunderstand each other   with understanding
the shape of those words   notwithstanding

6. Where do you intend to live in Canada?
a) Province/Territory b) City/Town

the house is a nest in a rotting tree

decorating the landscape
erupting from an acorn
collected at the town square

a mourning dove

nests in crushed empty diet orange soda cans
softened with crinkly honey bun wrappers
blowing from a gas station trashcan

the craggy satisfaction of turkey vultures

mix with chimes of cars
driven through spitty gasps of deer
finding the stench of a dead thing

moss-like nests

falling on the ground
hanging for only a few more moments

a live oak branch

stricken with a bolt to hold a child's first swing
and lightning

PERSONAL DETAILS

1. Full Name

Family name(s) (exactly as shown on your passport or travel document)

Salmon (*still. see also 2b*)

Given name(s) (exactly as shown on your passport or travel document)

When you name your daughter a name that is not linked to you
not Italian not carrying the history of her father's people
not your grandmother's name not your grandfather's name
that was his grandfather's name that was his grandfather's name
that was his grandfather's name that was his grandfather's name
that is the name you give your son

Holly When you name your daughter after a non-familial invasive plant
painful to brush against deadly to fall into prickly and poisonous
spreading wild in a new province like immigrants always do

When you repeat the last syllable of her name with the first
syllable of her middle name without even acknowledging the
strange rhythm will always be one repeated syllable off from being
immortalized somewhere say in that Boston song her high school
boyfriend played once again as the battery drained from his
custom-painted Nissan Sentra parked at the end of your cul-de-
sac in the hours before curfew and always a few minutes after
because she needs you to stop treating her like a child

When her name will always sound southern and hardly ever quite literary but reminds you somehow of your little sister whose name you will say instead sometimes and more often as you age

You will know then the name is ready to engrave on her life.

2a. Have you ever used any other name (e.g. Nickname, maiden name, alias)
[ ]*No [ ] *Yes

all of the reasons I did not use to change my name
I am not remembering now as I fill out this form
one box after one box tick tock warning
        change of gender
        adoption
        domestic abuse
        witness to a crime
        parent's remarriage
        parent's abuse
please remember in a nonemotional way
the box demands
how much this made you the you we are evaluating
        while staying the you you have
hung   yourself to become

2b. If you answered "yes" to question 2a), please provide the name (e.g. Nickname, maiden name, alias, etc.)

Family name(s)

Flauto
the birth name is the name
lost dropped with callous pleasure
real name maiden name
squandered name original name
family name this name
my name name name

Salmon
the someday-on-this-list name
is not trout but Salmon
unbound when I love you
indefinitely is engraved
on the teenager
unwounded from   himself
and his dad's worn-sharp gnawing
on that umbilical cord

Chong
I do not need to tell you reader how a second marriage is one approached having learned a couple things about what it means to take someone else's name all of a sudden your own and trap yourself in your mistakes or lack of foresight or loveblindness or an established email username so this is not my last name even

though sometimes in two nations of white checkboxes I ever so secretly wonder if it could be until I remember the whys it is not

Flalmong
the Hollywood blend created
just for this house
to sort all of it under
used without permission
from the sorted

Given name(s)

Noel
embroidered in felt letters
on the back of my stocking
second choice after Crystal

Andy sewn on my brother's back

the homesick week every year
December 22
I lie and the barista embroiders Noël
on the back of my cup
with a sharpie
same same

Andy is Angelo again
for professional reasons
and a relative scale of relatable ethnicity

Le'anne
apostrophe lost
older cousin Le'Shea's Le'postrophe
the envy of us all and of course
borrowed into my signature
between eleven and seventeen and
maybe fifty-one and sixty

3. UCI

clear dockside instructions
for Ellis Island immigration officers

Race or people to be determined
by the stock
from which the aliens sprang

I am descended from stock
sprung from stock
emerged from stock

and the language they speak.
Mother tongue is to be used
only to assist

my mother tongue Texan
laced with an adherence to
grammar-school grammar
proper in a Southern sense
systematically racist in another

in determining
the original stock.

my stock from which I sprang
whole and person sprung
spring emergent

4. Sex

I long for they/them
can be me/me

I act he/him
at work
conference badges not withstanding
though everyone else sees she/her

I fail when the perception of disconnect
is still real this year

at home maybe a they/them
with a they/them
mostly she/her
until the back-gate breaks

I adapt he/him
as I carry the valentine's day
toolbox present from my she/her
to my he/him

I become tangled in the stereotypes
of the drill even when I set the letters

5. Height (cm OR ft. in.)

our fathers fell despite strong grasps
                                                            hands held
                                                            tethers strong
one after another
remembered in essays
                                            poems
                                            memoir
in stories
    conversations
    tears
recognized outside ourselves
our dead fathers mattering
one before another
                                                        falling
on concrete
     bricks
     gravel
grieving into quarry-cut marble
                                                                marshmallows
watched our mothers rage
                                                        wither
                                                        give away closetfuls
            pressed baby blue dress shirts
            yellow polo shirts
            white socks in new packages
we held on to scraps and icebergs
      donned his robe

drove his car
carried his cell phone in our back pockets
handkerchiefs in handbags
pajamas folded in a box under our bed
marginalia of memory
our mothers took off their rings
sometimes in the garden
became women we did not know
in their sidelines their space our space
filling the empty space full of the writing

6. Eye Colour

identity is a photo now where we find meaning

as a teenager I had a fake ID

I had green eyes a different name

I wish I could remember my birthdate

I knew my sign Pisces just in case

the bouncer noticed the non-green eyes

full of lights: coors keystone bud

full of the insecurity of what sixteen brings

and the pull of the need to drink

to take a risk

but then I did and now I need to

but I could never have the eyes for it

7. Date of Birth

Independence-
day in my birth-
country is my half-
birthday celebrated every year with fire-
works compliments of tax-
payers and cup-
cakes compliments of my mom who knew first-
hand what a post-
christmas birthday celebration-
occasion was not so cup-
cakes and fire-
works and one year a bottle of nail-
polish in a red-
shade called Go.

8. Place of Birth

I from Kentucky and he
writing a book about racehorses
a certain sign toward the meetcute story
when we collided

my birthday a gap of four days
from every thoroughbred birthday
in the Northern hemisphere
made me the one

without me
he went to Kentucky
claimed a crystal trophy shaped like a penis
for his galloping prose

9. Citizenships(s)

when my country closed its borders to people in pain
I was already on the other side of the wall

my view through a chink in the mortar
voices only sometimes

I didn't understand
        the life they were living
I understood
        how history happens
        how everyone sits in sugary syrup
        until too caramelized to move

the people who are good and know better
killed in front of children
sucking on sticky sour rosemary branches

when my country kept its borders open to people who are ill
I was still on the other side of the way

my view expansive
news and news and fear and an uncle who died
my mom's youngest brother
                                        and an uncle who died
my dad's youngest brother

delays in processing of paperwork
meant I couldn’t visit my mother
when she broke her foot in two places
slipping on a magazine or some mail

10. Current country of residence

Four months and seven weeks ago
my mom came to visit
a dad not my dad at the swing set
introduced himself polite neighbourly
"Where are you visiting from?" "Texas"
she said smiling my mom
"I'm sorry" he said
then there was me
standing on the slide speaking
a declaration about his pitiful geographicalism
pigeonholing my place
insisting this country be what I need
"1-2-3 Swinnnngggg!"
let my mother love her home
— where my dad lies still —
like I love you
I mean mine

my americanness sliding into
the bases of my playground
Canadasburg address

11. Date and place of your last entry to Canada

I carry peanut m&ms tied in leaf-green bundles to my mother
at the airport hide my questions and story of the tobacco
planted next to my peas she shows me rosemary prickly pear
lantana spearmint behind deer nets in her backyard

my two-leafed nightshade paid for by the ministry in the box
right outside my teenage son's window miles away the baby
a plant to take home for stopping work and being present
at a catered salmon dinner no bannock and rooftop planting

sweet grass wild strawberry columbine alliums my bluegrass
roots demanded tobacco the gift given to elders the offering
you bring in respect to open a conversation to ask a question
to make a request the acres of questions are a states-worth

think about your request I read as you tie up the leaves fresh
or dried in a pouch as you tie it correctly in red yellow green
or blue cloth and twine offer it in your left hand state
your request clearly with plenty of time to wait and listen

in daydreams and nightdreams I tie packets for my ancestors

for my father I wrap up liquorice in yellow
for Nanny blue twine knotted around slips of bible verses
for Nani paper too in reams perfumed like romance novels
wrapped in lasagna

12. Previous countries of residence: During the past five years have you lived in any country other than your country of citizenship or your current country of residence (indicated above) for more than six months? [ ] *No [ ] *Yes

I have lived here long enough
to distinguish
big umbrella weather purse umbrella weather
galoshes weather raincoat weather
umbrella galoshes and raincoat weather
to know
those few rainy days to skip everything
to have
lost three umbrellas
and refound one
to walk by and leave
countless others
I may or may not yet know

I have lived here long enough
to love the bus
learn the winter the summer routes then
to miss my car
to hear my order
as I walk into the coffeehouse on the block
small london fog?
then the next coffeehouse years later
single-shot latte?
years pass again
decaf cortado?

I have lived here long enough
to remember
my yellow American-sized kitchen
where I hung
the copper basket of garlic and onions
instead of outside on the balcony

too late in the season
where I reaching for garlic
got stung by a wasp
a sting received

before I lived here long enough
to know
how the wasps hang on
long past when the late summer salmon
is eaten at a picnic table on the balcony
or later backyard

to know
it was not too late
in the season
for wasps

13a. Your current marital status

my connoisseur of bourbons
burning and sweetness
smoke
musty and musky
spice and fermentation

to my love
on the occasion of eight months after your birthday
which is also now our anniversary
because you love me even though

we met in a valley of mine
on a mountain of yours
together damming a river
into a city reservoir

cry me a lake
I did
whirlpools appeared on dinner dates
droughts imminent
tracks everywhere

leaving the warm whiskeyness of bed
to walk a mother's dog
and return
obligations and eyelids heavy
wet and dripping

a hot walker then
a groom later
sweat rained into the dust and mud
concrete sidewalks and limestone paths

whimsically sublime and wantonly flexible
firmly yourself
attracted to understanding the immersion
in a world only sort of like your own

13b. (If you are married or in a common-law relationship) Provide the date on which you were married or entered into the common-law relationship

three months after his dad died
we got married

Three Dudes Winery
on the banks of the San Marcos River
three kinds of bad wine
and the best barbecue brisket in the world

I held a bouquet of daisies
special-ordered from the grocery store
peppered with bay leaves
selected from the tree in the backyard

we looked at the tree from the family room
where three of us sat in those last moments

three months before my dad died
we got married

13c. Provide the name of your current spouse / common-law partner

Family name(s)

I love when he says his name
with ringing syllables

he admonishes me when I try

my daughter says it now
as many times as I ask her

Given name(s)

he has an English name
and a Chinese name from his father
like my daughter
she has an Italian name after my father's English name
and a Chinese name from his father
another path another way an alternate road
that was mapped to her
before we knew she was going to be

14a. Have you previously been married or in a common-law relationship? [ ]*No [ ]*Yes

this section requires the

Declaration
For Non-Accompanying Parent For
Minors Immigrating to Canada

A short form I secured with an offer
to pay the child's father the fee
I had to pay the lawyer for a waiver

he provided the forms allowing
my our son to stay here with me as a

Without Both Parents or Guardians

which in the clarity of now seems dimes
for him to sign a document stating
he acknowledges
this child is unlike and like
him both shh I cannot thank him enough

14b. Provide the following details for your previous spouse / common-law partner:

Family name(s)
Darcy, or Salmon

Given name(s)
B. when I met him legally W. Noel
I thought that was a sign
for a brief period of self-honesty
short W. then a shorter more pretentious W.
and now maybe B. again
Wb. in my contacts if you can't help
but contact him

please understand now he
has already told me all this is ex-
aggerated and I misunderstood
my way is not how it happened he
never said that and he never hated
Canada I am imagining things
overstating vengeful failing and ex-
asperating misremembering and
manipulative obviously in
a midlife crisis and counselling is a
trick I use to get my way and he is
worried about me and wanted to help
I need to leave this Canada for my
own good I spoil our child so completely

14c. Type of relationship

the list of reasons my ex-husband might
have said he hates Canada

I live here
Guns are illegal Possession of fireworks
is only allowed with a permit and
on Halloween Boys can have emotions
strong erupting emotions visible
emotions whoa other people see them
and know them and react with other
emotions Homosexual marriage
is so fucking legal rainbows emerge
everywhere held up by everyone forced
under his feet at the crosswalks People
are cold People are too dependent on
social resources All the weather is
dreary There's no river in the middle
of town to swim in Wine is expensive
Gender is fluid Ice cream is super
expensive Taxes are high The awful
his word apartment we waitlisted for
was scuzzy his word We waitlisted for
everything Books are expensive Literature
here is sub-par The Giller Prize hardly
stands up to Pulitzer or National
Book Award writing Most Canadian
authors are not worth reading Ondaatje
excepted The university is

podunk The scholarship in English and
Linguistics is too focused on social
issues The pizza is bad My friends are
not good enough even the Americans

14d. From / To

over dinner one evening another
road trip the American southwest
I
make eye-contact
and inside those blue eyes
flash of evil fleeting wave
of nausea
subliminal flash
but not because I
noticed liminal
and ask him "do I
like trout?" and he
"how the hell do I
know?"
and then become afraid of ordering
the meal
the trout I
might not like and still
a few months later we marry
trout uneaten
Albuquerque lost
warning forgotten

the agent said I
got every date wrong
in boxes on

the Consular Report
of Birth Abroad of a Citizen of
the United States of America

the year
the date married
the date divorced
I

archived some files in twenty-ten
I

apologized to the American
citizenship approved even while my
memories devolved
with flashed warnings
the agent heeds like I
with the damn trout

this is true to the best of my knowledge

14e. Date of Birth

I imagine a sofa overrun
thrown pillows cross-stitched and carried by mail
to my ex-husband on American
holidays like the one my half-birthday
Alienation is real   Expertise
is acquired   Life throws curved snowballs Home
is where home is   Survival sometimes means
compromise   What's best for the together
is sometimes harder for the alone   Self-
loathing is non-transferable except
to children   Mistakes become secrets when
you use your belt to fix them   The ideal
man is not Marlboro or gaslighting
My home or country   is not your country
Canadian authors rock my   world

CONTACT INFORMATION

Current mailing address

you are the lady next door
and you have committed suicide

your husband disappeared for a month
then reappeared

alone
like me

like all of us new to the city new to the country
like you

I knew him but didn't know him
know him

I didn't know what to say when I saw him
I knew you both

like you know your neighbours
in the city new to the city

instead I saw you every day
and didn't know you at all

like we all know each other
new to the city

if you were my best friend
I would know what to say

when to call
I would know the right time to knock on his door

or use my key you lent me
when I watered the plants

I would know where you are buried
where your funeral was

why you died how you did it
what your father was like

in my dreams now
you had been my best friend

you are my best friend
we meet in the evenings

we had babies at the same time
then moved to separate suburbs

you send pictures
we get together again and again

sometimes
awkward and comfortable

we spend a summer together on a lake
the so-tall-now kids playing together

almost drowning together
like they had just seen each other yesterday

together
we have the right goodbyes

the tears the hugs the laughing
the we'll-come-visits

a balanced goodbye
at the end

I should ask the man next door
if you said goodbye

if he cried
if you cried

if you tried to call me and I didn't answer
if you knew

if you dream of me too

Residential address

Fade in.

Narrator:
this is the fourth garden I have rented
fifth if you count the summers we shared
a plot in a community garden
on an estate-turned-city-park

Dissolve

Act One
Ext. New Haven, Summer 2005

a house down the block from the owner   remarried
a front flower bed planted over years
butterflies peanut shells and perennials
bloomed one after another in a planned chaos
crocus daffodil daylily Echinacea poppy peony daylily
roses outside the kitchen window
my work dividing and replanting and giving away

Dissolve

Intermission

Ext. Vancouver, raining, 2008

a courtyard full of discarded plastic toys
slide playhouse playhouse broken car broken truck
from all the former tenants of eight apartments
there for a semester or a few years
I organized a cleaning party
made a friend and an enemy
planted strawberries in a pot by my front door

Dissolve

Act Two

Ext. Vancouver, sunny Fall day, 2010

shared use of the backyard
loved until the house was sold
to a woman who misunderstood trellised grapes or peonies
cut them down instead of staking them
the bamboo did well
she missed the rhubarb

Dissolve

Act Three

Ext. Vancouver, Spring 2011

a shared yard again
the owner moved out with her boyfriend

I made a rock garden in the front
from pieces I found behind the shed
pulled out the hostas I loathe
added rosemary to the herb garden
planted poppies I caught a woman pulling out
when the for sale sign went up

Dissolve

Act Four
Ext. Vancouver, Summer 2016

a neighbourhood alive with bubble tea
lobster rice and oranges
all the eyebrow threading
I will never need
a yard née yoga studio
a three-storey hedge
green like everything
sheared one summer
while my tears watered
herbs and peas in the garden box

with terrorist stealth
I plant four kinds of mint in the flower beds
when I move out

Fade out

End

PASSPORT

1. Do you have a valid passport/travel document?
[ ]*No [ ]*Yes

there is no photo of my great-grandmother
rilasciato Angela Natte il 2 Ottobre 1895
on her passaporto identity based on a series
one-word characteristics on page two

Statura	*m1.57*	
Eta	*anni 15*	
Fronte	*regolare*	
Occhi	*castagni*	imagine chestnut
Naso	*greco*	like the character in that book last year
Bocca	*regolare*	
Capelli	*castagni*	
Barba	/	
Baffi	/	
Colorito	*roseo*	rosy as 15 should always be
Corporaturo	*regulare*	what choices beyond regulare could there be?
Segur Particolari	*n*	

2. Country of issue

permission to travel for my great grandmother
was given by the Second to Last reigning King of Italy
permission to escape his reign to Cleveland

permission to travel for me
given under the depersonalized authority of the department of state
with no intrinsic permission but to come back

permission to travel to my mother's house
sell the cake pans stored in the garage hall closet pantry
from years of birthdays anniversaries and good-bye parties

3. Issue date – Expiry date

I long for this collection
in the file cabinet or firebox
the passports without photographs
where the words mean everything
along with the others already there
the ones with baby photos
            and 5-year-old photos
            and 10-year-old photos
the ones with permission to travel
            regular blue and diplomatic burgundy
            almost identical stamps they will not explain
the ones where I barely recognize myself as me before

Eta	*anni* 42
Fronte	small and furrowed
Occhi	deep brown worried pools
	the right bigger than the left
Naso	strong enough to introduce a heedless
	"where is your family from"
Bocca	small lips look crooked with lipstick
Capelli	classico long wavy and thick with white
	let's say highlights
Barba	one stubborn hair on the right side
	underneath my chin sometimes
Colorito	cheeks pigmented from a recent pregnancy
Corporoturo	milk-filled breasts out of proportion with hips
Segur Particolari	concerned with the social repercussions of

	describing woman's bodies for identification
	purposes and the state of the world and in love
Eta	*anni* 20
Capelli	chin-length cut perfectly angularly
	smelling of other people's cigarettes
Occhi	eyes searching dark bright eye-liner heavy
Bocca	small but pursed confidently
Corporoturo	gin-dependent dressed for retail work
Segur Particulari	where will I dance tonight
Eta	*anni* 15
Capelli	JCPenney curls washed dried and hot-ironed
	daily
Occhi	black devil eyes
	said the random boy in the cafeteria
Fronte	clear small tenacious
Naso	oh no! it actually says Grecian?!
	I look like a weird bird
Corporoturo	spidery with a short torso and skinny arms
	reaching out farther than they should
	but not as far as they are capable
Segur Particulari	dreams only of Nobel prize winners
	and Danielle Steele romances

NATIONAL IDENTITY DOCUMENT

I wanted to go to this party
with no invitation
super cool place
I asked a person I knew
they knew a person who was going
that person said sure the more the merrier
the people who lived there
did not know about us
or about the party
they ran out of food
water space to sit
we didn't

the person I came with and I
we took the art off the wall
shipped to a friend of mine an academic
with a grant
we left with the silverware
carved our names in the floors
stole the walls
I asked the person is this ok?
can I take this?
they said sure
so I did
they said to leave a note
let the people know
leave my name

my knife thrust in the tree trunk exclaiming
what is mine

a few months later we went back
choose a bedroom
the person said
whichever you like
we would live in the house
now
they would live in the shed
they are used to this
they camped
for summer vacation last year
we send their kids off to school
to learn to become better
at living in the shed
at respecting our authority
at eating without silverware
at producing art for my friend with the grant

we rename the place
after our fathers to honour them
gain approval they never gave us
we invite friends to share
our ensuite bathrooms
to sit on the deck facing away from the shed
see the setting sun
appreciate how beautiful a place this is
we say is ours and settle

EDUCATION / OCCUPATION DETAIL

1. Highest level of education

I will start the recording.

Do you work?
Yes. Should I say more?

What is your work?
I teach writing. English.
[Laughter]

What is your highest level of education?
Masters degree.

In what?
English.
[Laughter]

Who examining whom,
she checks all the boxes on a form in her binder.
Is it my vocal fry or my upspeak?
unveiling the expertise.

What is your favourite day of the week?
[Laughter]

2. Number of years of education in total

Derrida's
replacement
shattered
tower
after
city
of
blue

discarded
the mess
from the top
out of sight

put the blocks
from the bottom
on top
close

stared

moved an entire arm
in colorless mimicry

grew heavy
as I grow
tired or
intellectually
overwhelmed

3. Current occupation

I fell victim
you followed your script
she victim of him
I victim of her
he victim of her too
you victim of me of you of her of him
I victim of you
I am the silent victim
one of them
the one whose survival
whole being
ebbing the ebbs to survive the flowing
depends on believing
the victim
I am the victim
I am the survivor
I survive because of you
because you believe the victim
you are surviving
I need you to trust me
I need you to say you understand

who is the victim
you ask me
my answer
a victim so different
than the one you think

you are taught
you believe
unquestionably
your predator
insatiable luring smooth devouring
full of façade
victim among victims
evidence of what
the life of a victim
the ability to perpetrate
she assumes my identity
a warning
weaves
a Nick to her Gatsby
while I fall in hopelessness
I try my voice
and choose silence
I hear you say listen to the silence
but not my silence
he falls
not in love
shiver shake
becomes a shell of skin
the bane card
is silence
the fault line a tunnel
the quakes only shuddering
of her cold shoulders

we victim together
crushed by the post of the house
surviving our dynasties
and thrown in the bin with the silent masses

4. Intended occupation

walk and write and gather the facts
        not the composition
        every day the same poems the same place
        the same chair the same drink of the week
        on stolen time
                snuck it
                hid it
                stored it for winter
        each moment recorded in case
        pencil pen crayon lipliner in the park
the moment still unwritten
        distracted and free
        written with every detail
        at the end of the notebook
        the facts run back
        fit but not belong
and the poet looms
        grocery lists
                bananas eggs milk chx five-spice powder
        flawed directions
        couplets
        notes
                lectures tours readings
        schedule of errands
                to you re: summer
        memory of cigarette smoke on balmy days
        slice of life
                man on bicycle water bottle
you fell asleep in your ars poetica

LANGUAGE DETAIL

1. Native language / Mother Tongue

my mother tongue is a series of words
phrases
conversational characteristics
talk about feelings
lawn chair psychology
forthright and wrong observations

my mother tongue is a little cutting
and adds an extra emphasis
on the final syllabic ‘p’ in

yep

and especially

nope

2. Are you able to communicate in English or French?

I can identify 廣東話
especially dimsum related words: congee, one of
the word for father's mother
that sounds like the toddler word for me
but I worry about using the characters here
it's not my language

I can say my husband's last name in 廣東話
but my inability to get the tones right
embarrasses me and makes me giggle
and I learn not to do that
but I worry about using the characters here
it's not my language

my husband's mother tells him his 廣東話
is terrible and my son uses his chopsticks
with more skill and is more handsome
and I learn "I love you, son"
I know this language

and then "I love you, grandson" in 廣東話
when she tells a nosy waiter the reason
her blue-eyed grandson does not look like her
is because he dyes his hair a very natural-looking
dark blonde
I know these characters
I know this language too

3. Have you taken a test from a designated testing agency to assess your proficiency in English or French?

They took everything from me
at the check-in desk
I gave them everything I brought with me
"We will give everything back to you
afterwards"
at the Turkish bathhouse
they give you a robe
bunny-soft on your naked shoulders
a place to put everything and a key

you are bare and warm
steamy and indulgent
scrubbed raw and rubbed soft again

here instead we lined up
so many colours
vinyl on our passport covers
we showed them
—-those frowns those scowls—-
we showed them our empty hands
empty pockets
"We need to check under your head covering"
the man in front of me lifted his turban

and they looked inside his empty ears

"Lift your hair up please"

they said to me (me!) next

"We need to check your neck"

I did I was afraid
what would they find on my neck
my hair is thick so thick and heavy
long and brown and so thick
some strands of grey already
weight lifted from my shoulders
my neck cold exposed

"ok"

empty too

DEPENDANTS — PERSONAL DETAILS

you are planning on becoming
pregnant a second time

now that you are in Canada
your third child

statistically two-thirds of a third

who would have been born in America
will not be born

ever
will not crawl

pretend to be a brachiosaurus
require yet another parent-teacher conference

one anchor baby is enough
and you will make a choice

a birth plan others will shame
you will frame as necessity

scandalously elective
and as sanitized as a scheduled flight

you will welcome your baby
from your sliced womb straight into your arms

and to your breasts
then days later

home
you have years together until

your anchor baby
is shot

at school
with her classmates

lined up in the gym or cafeteria
you are not there with her
to hold her hand
or put her to your breasts again

where she is yours and yours alone
and not there

she will be brave
on her own

push up her sleeve
look right at the needle

and into the eyes of the school nurse

enter now bullet-size tears
salt and shrapnel

in memoriam
your two-thirds

of the third baby
grown so tall

and killed in his classroom
in America

SCHEDULE A
BACKGROUND / DECLARATION

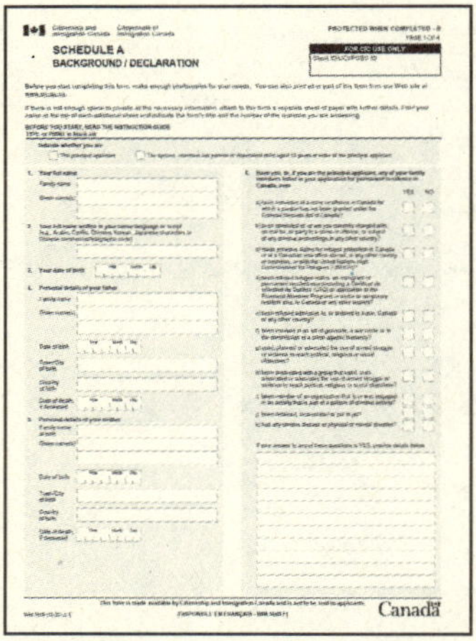
SCHEDULE A
BACKGROUND / DECLARATION
Canada

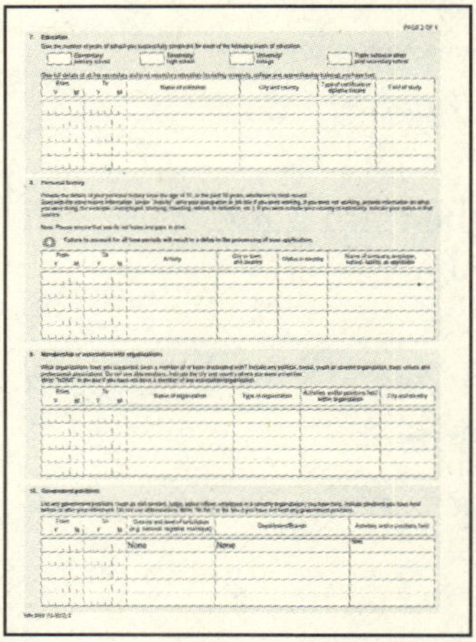

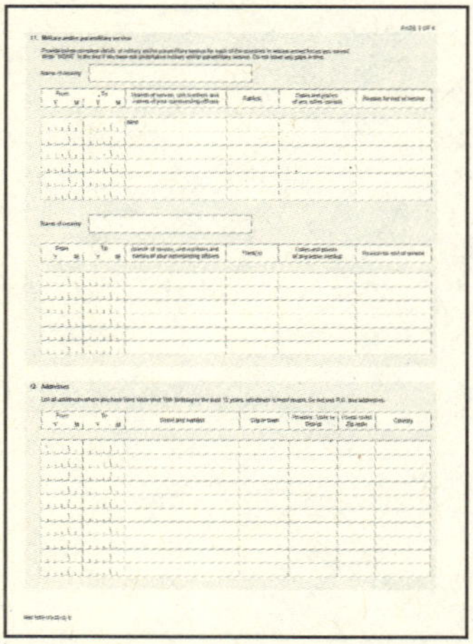

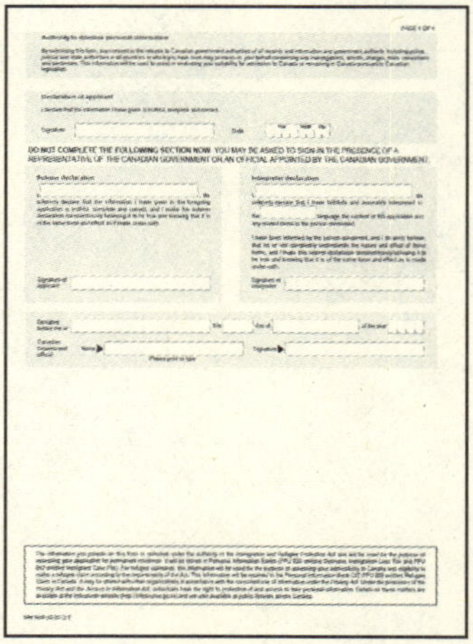

I. Your full name

I discovered crystals again
thanks to a need to protect myself at work
black tourmaline a cold chest plate
rocks filled my pockets
heavy memories

I found the collected stones of my travels
and understood my wish-name was grounded
in more than a veneer shine
solid femininity scientific fractal protection
only to those who understand why

I spent my salary and all my pocketspace on rocks
and now find them all over me

under the bed
tucked on shelves
in drawers
baskets
my daughter's coat pockets

2. Your full name written in your native language or script

I am ahistorical a signpost
a mid-70s middle-class middle-of-the-road aesthetic

common enough to know what my life is like
a character in a script for a new teen drama series reboot

not common enough to appear on a license plate
at the Cracker Barrel or a pencil as I exit the gift shop

3. Your date of birth

Camus died on a Monday
on my birthday
fifteen years before
my birth a Saturday's child

relevant because *The Plague*
was rewritten at a desk above my bedroom
when I was 42 years old

American emigrant TS Eliot died
on my birthday
and on that same day
Michael Stipe was born

relevant to my jealousy that he not me
may be the poet reincarnated

4. Personal details of your father

Family name

the flute charm around his neck I remember him buying in Bogota
when he died his oldest grandson did not share his name
the next oldest grandson was offered
and then I realized
it was my brother who treasured it most
and wears it now
without the guilt of my oversight

Given name(s)

my dad was second generation and third generation
Cleveland-Italian
Frank because Sicilian grandfather Francesco
he loved to add his initials to everything
FJF Frank Jerry
when I was middle-aged and he was dying
we found his birth certificate
Frank Gerry after Garibaldi
FGF
life is never as straightforward as I
imagined he thought

5. Personal details of your mother

Family name at birth

I write Edge here with envy at the coolness
and act offended when someone says
"Don't get too close to the Edge."
and for a while correct everyone like my mother does
"Can I?" "I don't know, can you?" "May I?"

Given name(s)

her name too like his mother's was Jenny
but always Jenny
born of a family who could be traced
out of Texas all the way to Tennessee generations ago
but no further
English probably

I spit in a tube to understand
their Virginia Colony colonizer story
indentured servitude for a new life
her childhood Christmas stocking used the more colloquial
JenniLee

6. Have you, or, if you are the principal applicant, any of your family members listed in your application for permanent residence in Canada, ever:

a) been convicted of a crime or offence in Canada for which a pardon has not been granted?

b) been convinced of, or are you currently charged with, on trial for, or party to a crime or offence, or subject to any criminal proceedings?

c) made previous claims for refugee protection in Canada or with the United Nations High Commissioner of Refugees?

d) been refused refugee status, an immigrant or permanent resident visa or visitor or temporary resident visa, to Canada, or any other country or territory?

e) been refused admission to, or ordered to leave, Canada or any other country or territory?

f) been involved in an act of genocide, a war crime or in the commission of a crime agains humanity?

g) used, planned or advocated the use of armed struggle or violence to reach political, religious or social objectives?

h) been associated with a group that used, planned or advocated the use of armed struggle or violence to reach political, religious or social objectives?

i) been a member of an organization that is or was engaged in an activity that is part of a pattern of criminal activity?

j) been detained, incarcerated or put in jail?

k) had any serious disease or physical or mental disorder?

If your answer to any of these questions is YES, provide details below:

"I'm really happy right now" she says crisp tones rising and falling
approximating valley girl radio DJ reality show contestant

I thought I had anxieties then I discovered real anxieties serious
and true and monitored lifelong struggles wars fought daily to
keep the anxieties away and away

I thought maybe I had anger issues I looked it up and realized
I totally did not have anger issues I threw fits and garlic and
laundry and insults and shade but not punches

I thought I might be depressed then depression seeped out
of the man who shared my bed draining away from me from
everyone dark and dreaded and absolutely alive and writhing

I thought I was in love love should be distinctive I saw others
in love love meant something else when I feel in love again
I know what love means and it is spectacular and warm

I thought I might be drowning but I knew how to swim so that
did not make sense except I was not swimming I was in love
"you don't actually think you are a swimmer" he said

maybe I wasn't? I forget
could I swim? I forget
would I drown? I forget that too

I thought I had memory trouble remembering conversations
wrong agreements never existing until I started writing down
revealing mine was solid black and perfectly dark and deep

I thought maybe I was a perfectionist someone told me to focus
less on the details and let things slide I didn't realize that is how
you defend yourself when someone else catches you slacking

I thought so many things until I started thinking in my own quiet
solitary and together not with them comfortable space of my own

"I'm really happy right now" he says dark with those sharp words
the tones rumbling the back of the sofa approximating nothing

7. Education

High School Diploma

Southeast Ohio coal mining belt university town
listed with America's top party schools
smoking menthol cigarettes to buy them from
that boy in my class who worked at the gas station

Bachelor of Arts

midwestern cornfields hiding a murder of farm boys
almost-engineers spending summers detasseling corn
pledged a sorority because mainstream gender roles
America in the '90s reigned for me
the men were never asked to dress in boobs and black
sing in paraphrase where every boy I crushed
every man knew not enough of future vernacular
rape culture awkward gropings no thank you ignored
                    beerblank spaces in memory
navigated from an accidental Cosmopolitan subscription
preceding a hope my children never timetravel
to know the feeling of leaving on initiation night
angry ex-boyfriends breaking windows
visiting the police station in the middle of the night
sorry I woke you up dad
one visit to the emergency room in the spring
for alcohol poisoning during grand prix week

Master of Arts
married to a guy who needed coffee to speak
the dishes done to engage
whose Texas-grown gender bias I only understand
after graduation five months pregnant
by a man with some wild-fig rooted mom issues
Cosmo never warned me about
mom expectations mom academic aspiration
unmatched to all the things he said
I was supposed to feel as a mother
in the few years I spent underwater

PhD? N/A
deferred acceptances yes multiples
to write a novel
to bring into the world another man
a man who embraces fluidity
and will likely never become a legacy
in his father's fraternity
as he learns to hold the narrative
on his side of the divide

8. Personal history

It's a full-time job.
That's the part I don't like.

It pays well.
For working my life away.

You are throwing away an opportunity.
I am sure that's what Juliet's mother said too.

She died.
I will too.

After you've wasted your life away.
Maybe before.

It's a heckalot of money.
To spend on Sunday afternoons at the mall? no thanks.

You could travel.
On my three weeks of vacation.

You'd have a title.
I prefer Rockstar.

Rockstar doesn't pay the car insurance.
It will.

Is that before or after?
You always assume a crash.

You need to set some priorities.
I have.

Feel good, follow your heart, it's so cliché.
I wasn't born with a silver spoon in my hand.

You won't die with one, either.
One of the many.

You need to say yes.
I've only said no.

At least consider it.
I have.

You'd get business cards.
To pass out at work.

To give to your friends.
They don't have pockets to put them in.

Are you going?
Yes.

I am glad you've listened.
Uh huh.

Let me know what happens.
With what?

When you tell them you are taking the job.
I'm not.

You said you were going.
I'm not going there.

9. Membership or association with organizations

the beautiful sweet baby pink roses
fence
the
climbed
cut
under the graft

now bloomed in boudoir magenta
in the mulch

music grafted on the soft movement
of
the
clouds
turning them grey

puffing them up in anger
annoyance

under a rented tent
conventioneers sat

divorcing them from a view
of the sky
a clang maybe beautiful
from the library lawn
a clang here

riling a booming cloud
lower in the sky
moving louder

a break

cool breeze abated

sun-blinded carilloneers creeping
from shelter
in search of sprouts wrapped in cardboard box

then the clouds lost blown westward
past the tower
swinging
north before the banging tune
bringing
the sunlight on sheets of music
illuminating
each
clang with precision

10. Government positions

brother and sister travelling together
    caged together
    under the seat

said goodbye to their parents
    their brothers and sister
    a twin brother

with the same extra toes
    tabby markings
    look of wonder in his eyes

I think we let them say goodbye
    forever goodbyes
    a foreign adoption

when the kittens came to Canada
    against their will
    after their rabies shots

I think I didn't ask them
    they travelled first class
    we got an upgrade

a stop at the agriculture desk at YVR
    next to the baggage claim
    "just one" the agent said

there were two
huddled so tightly together
to make one

a local here a stray cat with a story
greets them
through the sliding glass

once adopted and brought here before
she was not the cat
they expected her to be

I learned all that from
the tattoo in her ear
the call to the SPCA
a knock on several doors
a conversation with the lady
who abandoned her to the neighbourhood

now she stays in different people's houses
four or so food dishes
balconies and back porches

warm boxes filled with old towels
on two front stoops
that I've seen

from the baby pictures on instagram
I know the kittens were born
in a Jacuzzi tub

from photos too we learned a thing
    their first human father
    died

we plan to tell the kittens when they are too old to understand

11. Military and/or paramilitary service

viewed after death
if foreign born, how long
in U. S. A.? 47 years

when my dad was a year old
his grandfather 62 years old

Widowed
turned to Ash

four years after his wife died
was killed at work
in the Cleveland East Gas Company Explosion
killing 129 people
discriminating only by current location
the explosive element
leaked into the city sewer system
suffocating rats
flowing through the efficient
modern aqueducts
exploding all at once
then twice
a manmade urban volcano
hundreds of acres of neighbourhood gone
in a moment
he died at 10am
Sunday morning
two days later

immediate Cause of death
Thirddegree burn with Charring and

ashing
Industrial Accident
due to Failure
of liquid Natural gas
holders Nos. 3 and 4 with resultant
escape
of liquid Natural gas,
followed by fire on 10/20/1944

my dad's uncle died at work
a few years later
exploded in Germany
a fireball or firefight or firesomething
does it matter?

Killed In Action

son of an immigrant
fighting for America

my dad
son of an immigrant
American
career soldier
died

Cancer

and was buried with military honours
a few blocks from our family room
it is unclear if the mutations were caused
by environmental factors

Veterans who served anywhere
in Vietnam between January 9, 1962 and May 7, 1975
are presumed to have been exposed to herbicides,
as specified in the Agent Orange Act of 1991

or his work

12. Addresses

I know where I am
because I recognize
the taste of home
in the water

a metallic softness convinced me
rocky warmth in my mouth
finally
I was home
the taste
in the one moment
after I opened the tap
filled a glass
scratched with the dissolved sand
with water
drank

lungs are related to your skin
my acupuncturist says
you become sensitive when your lungs are out of balance
pores opening and closing
propped open and affected by everything
too many things enter
too quickly

at this pin on a map so far away from mine
the water is never completely cold from the tap
in this scorching summer section
the pipes run too close to the surface
too close to the insulating layers of limestone
that will always stay warm

the water tastes of the silt
layered in orange stains around the drains in the bathroom sink
clinging in greens to the inside of the water pitcher in the fridge
in the dullness of my hair
fossilized with minerals that will not rinse out

familiar like the smell of mouldy wood
at my grandmother's home
we put pennies on the railroad tracks in the backyard
my brother made smashed penny earrings
for my Christmas present

I wear them on burnished days
days when I need to feel
the heavy metallic pull of home
weighing on my ears

I am at home and the water
deposits a crust of lime on my skin
broken quartz scuttling in my lungs
suffocated by home

Signature

Did you snowshoe at Mount Seymour?
Was there a snowball fight?
Did Kevin hit your son with a snowball?
Did he throw a snowball back?
Do you like to play board games?
Was your first date at the racetrack?
Did you put $2 down on all the horses?
Did the long shot win?
Did you go to a bar afterwards?
Did you ever compare your relationship to a reality TV show?
Do you like pork chops?
When Kevin proposed were you wearing pyjamas?
Was it after a party you hosted?
Did you go get a manicure the next day?
When you got home, did he have flowers?
Was there a note for you in a (what is this game?) Dominion box?
Did it tell you to look behind you?
Were there two notes?
When did this happen?
When was your daughter born?
Did you have a c section early in the morning?
Did he wear a hair net?
Are you getting enough sleep?
Are you still in love?
Has John Lithgow ever bought you dinner?
Are you writing?

SCHEDULE 8
ECONOMIC CLASSES
CANADIAN EXPERIENCE CLASS

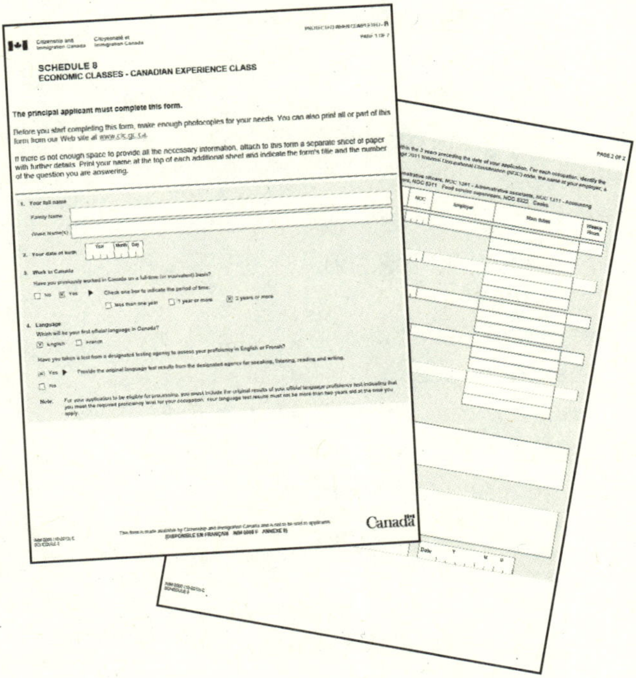

1. Your full name

I am revealed in an action
barrelling through a PTA I mean PAC meeting
or a committee at work
making decisions without the necessary consultation
choosing to act now and deal with consequences
later when or if anyone notices

Americanness all the way around

I do not integrate quietly
an elephant
a moose
a clydesdale in a maple syrup shop
no gentle giant
no sweet Kentucky belle
a hot-blooded racer
but you knew that when you hired me
when you should have chosen
a more-qualified Canadian

2. Your date of birth

my dad told me a story about my birthday
failure phrased as anecdote
born two days late instead of two days early
costing him an extra tax year
still no one considers me a bargain

3. Work in Canada

my immigration status this year a wrist twisted and broken by fear of existing without proper documentation I had coffee with a friend another American who revealed her secret an amputated hand to my tender arm her expired work permit

my work permit reminds me of an end MUST LEAVE CANADA BY [DATE] as soon as the new permit approved notice arrives the other renewal visits begin my social insurance number my health coverage my work health coverage sometimes my drivers license numbers and dates and forms tumbling like rocks riverbed of not frogs

my work permit insists I stay as I am UNLESS AUTHORIZED PROHIBITED FROM ATTENDING ANY EDUCATIONAL INSTITUTION OR TAKING ANY ACADEMIC PROFESSIONAL OR VOCATIONAL TRAINING COURSE so I can I teach those courses but cannot take them my educational institution listed above where I'm forbidden to take classes a professional and educational pause in a field where that pause maims

my work permit forces a violation and I hide and play NOT AUTHORIZED TO WORK IN ANY LOCATION OTHER THAN STATED and above shivering lock and key EMPLOYMENT LOCATION: UNKNOWN I remain silent in my undefined space a baby endangered in compliance while my work permit tries to save me NOT VALID FOR EMPLOYMENT IN BUSINESSES RELATED TO THE SEX TRADE SUCH AS STRIP CLUBS MASSAGE PARLOURS OR ESCORT SERVICES sex talk is not taboo on my work permit the thing that goes in my file at work temporary foreign workers are no longer eligible for jobs as exotic dancers officially defining work from work without telling anyone but the foreigners

while my work permit defines my role in the family NOT AUTHORIZED TO WORK IN CHILDCARE PRIMARY / SECONDARY SCHOOL TEACHINGS HEALTH SERVICE FIELD OCCUPATIONS my friend the one without the work permit chair of the PAC at her daughters' school she's a model mother her expired work permit whispering and protecting her keeping her safe as it twists tendons and tiny bones together under its thumb

4. Language

Which will be your first official language in Canada?

I am one quarter *Italiana* and no quarters *Italiana* speaking
my dad's grandmothers spoke only *Italiana*

Español came very easily for him
my mom's childhood proximity to the border of Mexico made
learning *Español* more difficult culturally and actually
yo hablo Español like a 13-year-old and I can text
jarringly with the babysitter

I know a smattering more *Français* gleaned
from my son's French-Immersion homework in
first and second grade
and by singing "*Au Champs Elysees*" in a continuing studies class

two semesters of 普通話
at the Saturday Chinese school
Where I learned to say Canada and pineapple
while my son learned so much more

I can count to *neununddreißig*
in *Deutsch* from a
British playschool in what was then West Germany
and I can order *pommes frittes*

My official language will be English

Have you taken a test from a designated testing agency to assess your proficiency in English or French?

to learn the Canadian sorry means to understand
an apology is a non-apology and an apology at the same time

to know the real apology and the excuse me apology
the forgive me apology

the apology that shames and inverts the shame

I am sorry I took over your land
but you were not using it to its full advantage

I am sorry I have not given it back yet
but that is complicated you know

I am sorry I have not called you
but you slipped my mind

I am sorry I bumped into you
but you were in my way

I am sorry I did not hear you
but I am listening to something more interesting now

that seems too harsh
my description American again

I did not mean for you to understand it that way
I am sorry

Provide the original language test results from the designated agency for speaking, listening, reading, and writing.

to understand the Queen is to be able to live in Canada
"The price of the gym membership is"
I waited
"two hundred and caikiouthy-four"
I didn't understand

I had to write an essay next
the value of art in the community
or should government fund art
or something politically dangerous
my thesis statement started with a yes
then three supporting paragraphs turned into a short story
I ran out of eraser but not time to rewrite
grateful I had not accidentally written a poem
as happens sometimes

in the middle of campus
in the middle of the city
in the middle of everything
the list of immigrants
my name
3:45pm

our speaking test

I met a man who took me down a back hallway
an elevator smelling like spoiled food
he pushed the buttons
Is this safe? I wondered
check your privilege
I told myself harshly even
                                        your journey your sacrifice
                                        is measured in papercuts

5. Your Work Experience in Canada

I met a futurist and it was not me yet

    with a microphone clipped to his collar
    he told us
what will what might what could or not happen
we are living in an era unprecedented
change the way we
in the history of the world
there are more than ever before
since the greeks
imagine a new kind of
neverbeforeness
blah blah blah
65% of the jobs for people who are toddlers now
do not currently exist

    over spaghetti with a fork in my hand
    I tell the teenager
there is a demand now for the creative class
theatre majors
with a friend or two
go on stage

    tell the audience what you learned
    on that subreddit last night
pepper in some "great thinkers" you admire
StalinMarx top poster on /showerthoughts

some words revolutionary technology unforeseen
and pioneering
        from your grandfather
if you don't know the answer
say something with confidence
        and me
be quick and cute and let them laugh with you in a way
they wish you would say what you just said again
unless they hate you already but they won't
because you are you

be sure not to stay past your best-before date

SUPPLEMENTARY INFORMATION YOUR TRAVELS

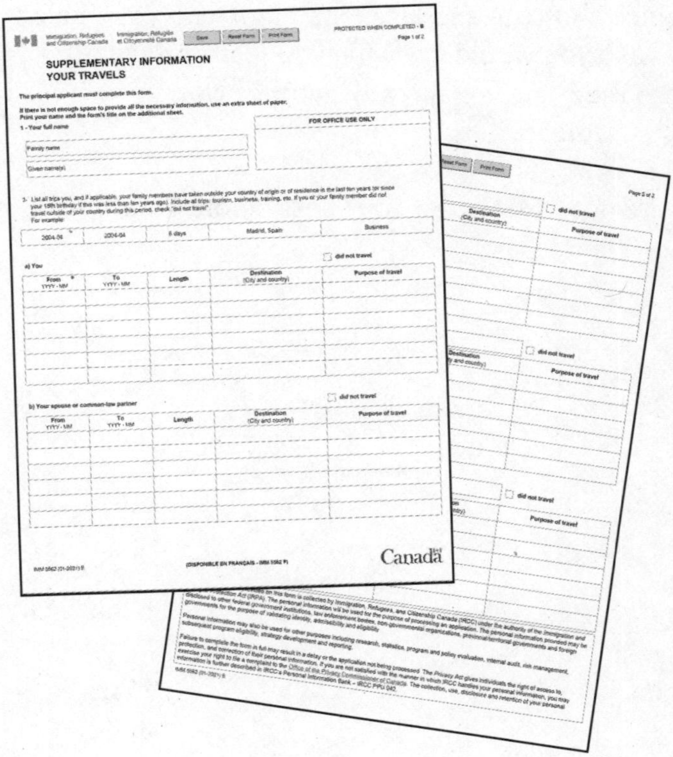

Immigration, Refugees and Citizenship Canada | Immigration, Réfugiés et Citoyenneté Canada

Save | Reset Form | Print Form

PROTECTED WHEN COMPLETED - B

Page 1 of 2

SUPPLEMENTARY INFORMATION
YOUR TRAVELS

The principal applicant must complete this form.

If there is not enough space to provide all the necessary information, use an extra sheet of paper. Print your name and the form's title on the additional sheet.

1 - Your full name

Family name

Given name(s)

FOR OFFICE USE ONLY

2- List all trips you, and if applicable, your family members have taken outside your country of origin or of residence in the last ten years (or since your 18th birthday if this was less than ten years ago). Include all trips: tourism, business, training, etc. If you or your family member did not travel outside of your country during this period, check "did not travel".
For example:

2004-04	2004-04	8 days	Madrid, Spain	Business

a) You — did not travel

From YYYY - MM	To YYYY - MM	Length	Destination (City and country)	Purpose of travel

b) Your spouse or common-law partner — did not travel

From YYYY - MM	To YYYY - MM	Length	Destination (City and country)	Purpose of travel

IMM 5562 (01-2021) E

(DISPONIBLE EN FRANÇAIS - IMM 5562 F)

Canada

1. Your full name

my government name yells in ALL CAPS
not me but my corporation
the one seeking solace here
in this country
non-sovereign status
trade me please
as the entity I represent

2. List all the trips you, and if applicable, your family members have taken outside your country of origin or of residence in the last ten years

My daughter, wrapped tightly to my chest, almost participated in what one of her biographers would describe as a watershed moment in terms of her activism and grit and kindness when she realized her mother would not be complicit.
I tell myself the other white woman did not notice the baby.

at the Vancouver airport
you   land
         go through customs
         claim your baggage before another customs checkpoint

all the planes converging from who knows where
you   wait for baggage together still trapped together
         behind a government-controlled glass door

so many people
shuffling closer to get our bags
shuffling back to pile them
         high on carts and on each other
         loaded with luggage soft-sided and hard-sided
         cardboard boxes marked with our names
         bags wrapped with layers of blue cellophane for security

maybe excited to be back at home from a long trip
              visiting fathers grandmothers brothers friends

maybe   replacing a mother's showerhead
adding a shelf in the kitchen for her birthday
cutting down a tree in the front yard whose branches were
  dangerously low
grazing the roof when she backed out of the driveway

maybe   arriving at this new home with culled possessions
  and overweight suitcases

maybe   a vacation away and back and now
  tired

"GO BACK WHERE YOU FUCKING CAME FROM"

I assumed the blonde woman meant me
then understood
  she meant not me
  she meant the luggage cart next to me piled high with boxes
  she meant the man in the turban at Carousel 17
    surrounded by his friends or family
    wife or sister daughters or nieces sons or nephews

then I said
I can't believe I said this

"That is not very welcoming"

my immigration status non-canadian for the record
and my mom-voice competing
with the squeaky wheels of the luggage carts
realizing only now I made assumptions about her and about him
and those were racist too

I probably should have said

"Don't be a racist bitch"

I could have said

"That was not kind"

"Be respectful"

or used the toddler-friendly strategy
ignore the aggressor comfort the wronged

then she came for me my white skin made me fightable outright
racially the punch easier than the verbal slap
and then her son

"Mom, it's not worth it"

held her back

maybe she was on the BEST vacation now coming back to work
maybe she visited her daughter who had married
a man from a land faraway and she missed her terribly
and wanted to scream

"COME BACK FUCKING HOME"

maybe her dad died and she had gone home for the funeral
or come home for the funeral

and she confused her sadness with anger
or lack of power like I do sometimes
while my daughter will not

Men, mothers, babies: all in her fucking way with all the baggage on all the carousels from who knows where all going around and around again.

ADDITIONAL FAMILY INFORMATION

Citizenship and Immigration Canada | Citoyenneté et Immigration Canada

PROTECTED WHEN COMPLETED - B

PAGE 1 OF 1

ADDITIONAL FAMILY INFORMATION

The principal applicant, their spouse or common-law partner (if applicable), and all dependent children 18 years of age or older must complete their own copy of this form. Complete ALL names in English and in your native language (for example, Arabic, Cyrillic, Chinese, Chinese commercial/telegraphic code, Korean, or Japanese characters). If additional space is required attach a separate sheet. **If a section does not apply to you, write "Not applicable".**

BEFORE YOU START, READ THE INSTRUCTION GUIDE. TYPE or PRINT in black ink.

SECTION A

Name	Relationship	Date of birth (YYYY-MM-DD)	Place of birth	Marital status	Present address
	Applicant				
	Spouse or common-law partner				E-mail address
	Mother				
	Father				

SECTION B **CHILDREN (Include ALL sons and daughters, including ALL adopted and step-children, regardless of age or place of residence)**

Name	Relationship	Date of birth (YYYY-MM-DD)	Place of birth	Marital status	Present address and e-mail address
					E-mail address
					E-mail address
					E-mail address
					E-mail address
					E-mail address

SECTION C **BROTHERS AND SISTERS (Including half - and step-brothers and sisters)**

Name	Relationship	Date of birth (YYYY-MM-DD)	Place of birth	Marital status	Present address

SECTION D **CERTIFICATION**

I certify that the information contained on this document is complete, accurate and factual. I also realize that once this document has been completed and signed that it will form part of my Immigration Record and will be used to verify my family details on future applications.

Signature: ______________________ Date (YYYY-MM-DD) ______________

The information you provide is collected under the authority of the *Immigration and Refugee Protection Act* to determine if you may be admitted to Canada as an immigrant. It will be stored in Personal Information Bank number EIC PPU 015. It is protected and accessible under the provisions of the *Privacy Act* and the *Access to Information Act*.

IMM 5406 (09-2013) E (DISPONIBLE EN FRANÇAIS - IMM 5406 F) Canada

Section A (Applicant, Spouse or common-law partner, Mother, Father)

Applicant

I emigrated in and out of Texas my mother's country not mine
then New Haven a city of presidents
where I did not belong but now I do
because I lived there long enough
then immigrated to Canada
the first of my family
following my then-now-ex-thankfully-partner for work
like so many others since met
a dream of a start to creating a better life
um
a dream of a step up for a year or two
a more privileged start than my young grandfather
where I could always of back home instead

Spouse or Common-Law Partner

my husband is a Canadian Citizen
immigrated to Canada age two
first and a half generation and 4th generation
his brother was born here and his great grandfather
paid the head tax and is buried here
in the same cemetery where we buried my father-in-law
just down the street from the house he lived in first
the house his uncle owned and happens to be almost next door
to the house we rented from the

lovely one-handed woman
who married a con

Mother

my mom was a career girl her words
                                        a snake sorry mom
                                        it's not me it's your year
when she met my dad
a representative for Lone Star Gas
teaching women how to use their new gas ranges
my mother's undergraduate degree
I do not know
I realize
I know her MA is in Home Economics
but I feel like I only know because
I am derisive

my maternal grandmother Geneva
did tailoring and made her clothes
and other people's clothes
but not my clothes
she and my mother made my mother's wedding dress
and more than likely a honeymoon outfit or two
I bought my wedding dress
made from recycled silk
from an eco-conscious designer's sample rack
in Canada
they took in the bust for me

I can cross-stitch and make Halloween costumes
mostly out of giant pieces of felt
I can make skirts with elastic waistbands
my best work is a laptop case for an 11-inch MacBook Air
made from a bargain bin leather scrap
on the 1943   year of the lamb
Singer sewing machine
my mom bought at an estate sale

her father was a cotton farmer
whose name was his initials: JW
after his father Joseph Winston
my mother's father JW also drove the school bus
rented land to plant cotton
walked to the Methodist church
while the rest of the family took the car
to First Baptist
where my grandmother Nanny played the piano
self-taught by ear
learned to read music eventually and worked
at the funeral home
after my grandfather died

my mom's name already on the stone
under the tree on the hill
next to my dad's
she does not like to go to church anymore
without him
she bakes muffins or lemon bars

and takes them to the welcome centre
for new families or travelling students making houses
for the poor like my dad did so often
then she leaves
stops by the cemetery
eats her lunch in the car
where she doesn't have to sit
by herself

Father

my Dad's family was Catholic
so was my Dad
a lamb
wanting to marry my mom
a southern Baptist who had a dinner
for prom in high school
instead of a dance
like footloose 1960-style
his religion said no her religion said no
plus racism he was I-talian
they are Methodists now
and were or will be buried a Methodist
we found his Saint Francis medal
in the safe after he died
alongside the dog tags and military medals
I do not know anything about saints or dogs

my dad fills so much
I stop here now

Section B CHILDREN

(include ALL sons and daughters, including ALL adopted and step-children, regardless of age or place of residence)

if I become a Canadian
I will be Gen First Canadian
the first Canadian in my family

my first was the only one anyone on my side
could remember ever having blue eyes

my second will be Gen Second
and Gen Second and a Half
and some other ordinal designation too
        mixed-generation is stunning

my first their half-brother
will be Gen First Canadian and Gen last letter too
        Gen Z
        Gen Active Reconciliation
        Gen Give Land Back and Move People Forward
my generation fallen behind

my first has been in Canada six years longer
than my Canadian second
an American Citizen of course
and still a Visitor to Canada

my first's father like my mother in this way and that
Gen X but not part Gen Empathy
frets tracing his family tree out of Texas
where his roots go deep his leaves are familiar
and where he thinks it is ok to not wear your seatbelt

my first is already old enough to understand
what this land is and is not to feel the longing of homes
the excitement of opportunity

my first is old enough to choose between being an immigrant
and ex-pat to choose differently than their father
or mother sometimes

my first's American half-brothers
Gen Undefined Unnumbered on their father's side
but only Gen Second on their mother's side
because my first loves them I in most likely misplaced
affection for those unmet boys list them here too

my second is named after their Italian-American grandfather
by their Chinese-Canadian grandfather
          mixed babies are stunning
Gen X racism cloaked in compliments and acceptances
becomes American when the certificate arrived in the mail

my second born in Canada has an American passport
I hold with mine when we travel together
and wonder if made the safe generational choice
for my sweet Gen Alpha child

Section C BROTHERS AND SISTERS

(Including half- and step-brothers and sisters)

I replaced my brother with broth

when I was young
we had a guard who followed us outside
my younger brother moved everywhere with me
we played mostly indoors that year

the next year we lived in a place cut out of a jungle
we turned his tricycle upside down into a grinding stone
made poison for the leaf-cutting ants
grinding up the flowers berries and leaves
adding warm water from the garden hose
in a malevolent soup
we carried giant nets
caught iridescent blue butterflies
snapped them the right way
to make their wings lie flat in the mounting
we framed them
and they moved with us
we swam sometimes
on days we felt brave
among the manatees
and fished
a small scar still on my cheek
where my brother hooked me once

instead of a bass
we cleaned the catch
on the front lawn
cut off their heads
watched their lips open and close
and helped cook the fillets
with sour orange slices

then for two years
we played like we imagined
small-town American children played
Cabbage Patch Kids GI Joes a swing set
a puppy named Licorice bicycles with friends
I won the Turtle Trot at the county fair
with a box turtle I found and then left
on the road by the woods behind the house

the puppy died from something
sometimes puppies get
so my brother chose two white mice
disappearing almost immediately
I chose a kitten with extra toes
who outlived my childhood
scowled at my first husband
who buried her in a grave
forced shallow by limestone and condescension

but before that
a new house in a new country

an outside wall again
peppered with lead sometimes
an occasional grenade
but this time luckily
not in our neighbourhood
the cat came with us after a brief quarantine
and we taught her to shake hands
we had two parrots in the living room
siblings or friends or lifelong companions
the maid was supposed to feed them
we were away for my grandfather's funeral
one pecked the other's eyes out
then died after we returned
loneliness maybe I have no memory of burying it

then high school an American college town
middle school for my brother
quick assimilation I thought
three years later my best friend told me
she thought I was an exchange student
who didn't speak English
my brother played football
became a boy scout a good authentic guy
we were in the same youth group at church
we were on the tennis teams
we became engineering majors
I moved away he stayed as long as he could
I am not an engineer

on vacations I search out the foreignness I miss
or I visit my mother to hold the thousands of souvenirs
too hard for her to part with
he seeks safe comfort
in American beach towns his memorabilia
Topps Upper Deck and Fleer remains sealed in boxes
in a childhood closet my mom complains he never calls
he has not yet met my baby now toddler
who reminds me of his youngest daughter
who people say reminds them of me

my mom sends me recipes
soups I remember eating with my brother
the bowls
Franciscan Ware Desert Rose
at the kitchen table my dad made
when they were first married
the table moved always with us
where we sat in those last moments
before my dad died
the memory I have of my brother
phone calls not withstanding
the herby taste of childhood soups
memories soggy with the weight
we share of all these things
our common childhood

Section D CERTIFICATION

I will be third generation American once-removed
mother to and daughter of a generation
once-removed

I was born in the year of the tiger
accustomed to inhabiting vast lands
I only bore lambs

she a wood lamb
he a water lamb like his grandfather
and step-grandfather
I only bore lambs

[IMMIGRATION FORM 2018B
APPLICATION TO LIVE ON THIS
LAND AS AN UNINVITED GUEST]

[redacted]

I acknowledge a missing checkbox
that is not a checkbox
because it is not that easy
though these forms weren't easy for me either
that's a different easy

did you speak to an elder
did you learn something
do you commit to a life of reconciliation

I make space for that unchecked box

no you were not involved
you are new here
but you too are a settler
and you come with a history of your peoples
your settler peoples

your elders
the ones whose words you did not hold
up and dear and true

the ones you cut off
the ones you told to stop speaking
the ones whose ideas were outdated
whose politics were old-fashioned
and racist

those elders
are your elders

you are a settler
a new settler
and you need to understand meaning
beyond the First People's Guide for Newcomers
written by settlers
in consultation of course

ask
acknowledge
admit
you are benefiting the same way the settlers did

you bring mispronunciation
instead of smallpox
misculturations
a once-removed twice-removed perspective
from the land
and a heavy stifling Americanness

DECLARATION OF APPLICANT

Canada:
I declare that the information I have given is truthful
complete and correct.

America:
I solemnly swear (or affirm) that the statements made
on this application are true
to the best of my knowledge and belief.

YOU HAVE A NEW MESSAGE IN YOUR CIC ACCOUNT

there is a park

where you sit in a shelter of driftwood
rebuilt every time you visit
when the orcas come to the shore
you can be sure they are only and obviously

walrus in disguise

this is where I landed

a bureaucratic anomaly housing the highest per capita
number of people in the witness protection program
on Canada Day weekend not the holiday exactly

the Saturday before

the tiny tip of America in Canada

where witnesses concentrate together hiding from something
or some stroke of luck incongruously sharing experiences
while unable to talk to anyone else

about the before-life

when you've lived there you know

for landscaping needs ask the notary for advice handling your
rebellious teenage daughter consult the clerk working day shifts
at the grocery store for advice on immigration

call the plumber

the uninformed

the new first grade teacher assigning a project
requiring baby pictures half the class came in empty-handed
some with babies cut out of magazines

blue eyes instead of brown

children completing second grade

bussed past eagle nests, blueberries and supportive
social-emotional curriculum across another landing spot
into a tiny bordertown to play high school football

as the Blaine Borderites

my Ellis Island

is where Canadians drive to pick up packages from Target
and the Container Store buy Tillamook cheese and $5 wine
that they may or may not declare

to the familiar officer

your immigration story paused

on Canada Day weekend you wrapped up my past identity
and stand still and walk the streets shared
with those Canadians who yet have not known to ask you

your questions

do you have regrets?

learning later you get a flag at the other landing
you wish you had gotten a flag but also not
because we don’t need it and you wouldn't have been able

to throw it away

Thank yous

Thank you to my friends and colleagues unnamed here who supported me along the way. You are embedded in these pages.

Thank you to the many writing groups where I've written beside so many amazing writers to work on these pages, at Liberty and Artigiano on Main Street, at ECUAD, at Douglas College, and at the Joy Kogawa House. Writing with you and talking about writing with you created this book.

Thank you to Rachel Rose, through the Vancouver Manuscript Intensive, for providing editorial feedback and confidence and inspiration. To Chelene Knight, who helped these poems move from such an early first draft to new shapes. To all my before-it-was-a-book readers, especially Liz Bachinsky, Fenn Stewart, Shay Wilson, with an extra special especially to Doretta Lau, for the reassurance, everything recommendations, sauna days, writing retreats, moral support and gossip.

Thank you to Liz, Chelene, Rachel, Doretta, Stephen, and Johanna for your kind and thoughtful words endorsing the book.

Thank you to Brian and Karen at Anvil for believing in this book and making it real! I am so thrilled to see my name on your lists of writers I admire.

Thank you to my kids. Joe, for the author photo (really too the time spend together on the walk taking the photo), the brainstorming and for being the inspiration that is you. Franny, for modelling what is is like to follow your ideas and goals with joy and confidence and sparkle.

Thank you to my family – my mom, my dad, my brother and family – for putting up with me as I found my way to me.

Thank you to Kevin Chong for everything: time, encouragement, believing, listening, the gift of VMI, finding an immigration lawyer when I needed one, and really just your steady unwavering kindness and love. And for that time at that literary festival when I held your bag for you to go on stage and you said you'd do the same for me someday.

About the Author

Surname: Flauto
Given Name: Holly [middle name redacted: not a poet name, see page 24]
Nationality: Newly Canadian; Secret American
Date of Birth: Capricorn, Sagittarius Rising
Place of Birth: As a poet? In a library, in a classroom, in a series of bedrooms and living rooms and bright spaces with naive confidence in those words that appeared on the pages.
Date of Issue: Fall 2024
Date of Expiry: 70 years following the end of the calendar year in which the poet dies

---

Holly Flauto is a poet, storyteller, writer, and learner. Their writing has previously been published in *The ex-Puritan, Joyland,* and *The Rusty Toque*. They teach English and Creative Writing at Capilano University. Originally from the US, Holly currently lives in Vancouver, BC.